The Modern Spirituality Series

Metropolitan Anthony
of Sourozh

The Modern Spirituality Series

Henri Nouwen

Metropolitan Anthony of Sourozh

John Main

Lionel Blue

Metropolitan Anthony

Metropolitan Anthony of Sourozh

A selection of his writing
and with an introduction by
Hugh Wybrew

TEMPLEGATE PUBLISHERS

First Published in 1987 by
Darton, Longman and Todd Ltd

BV
213
.B5
1988

ISBN 0-87243-167-3

First published in 1988 in the United States
by Templegate Publishers
302 E. Adams St., P.O. Box 5152
Springfield, IL 62705

Contents

INTRODUCTION

The Ecumenical Movement has, among other things, given rise to a growing interest in the Orthodox Church on the part of a significant number of Western Christians, not least in the Roman Catholic and Anglican Churches. Brought up in traditions which have to varying degrees encouraged an active life of Christian involvement, in which Martha has been more prominent than Mary, they have been attracted by a depth of spirituality which they have not always found in the contemporary life of their own Church. Such depths are most certainly there in the Western Christian tradition, as other books in this series testify. But there is no doubt that the Orthodox tradition has much to offer the Western Christian.

In apparent contrast to a good deal of contemporary Western Christianity, Orthodoxy has never ceased to insist on the primacy in the Christian life of prayer and worship, and on the necessity for both to be informed by Christian doctrine, to which in turn they give life. When this tradition is embodied in a Christian leader of the stature of Metropolitan Anthony of Sourozh, its appeal is strong. Those who have taken part in services celebrated in the Russian Orthodox Cathedral in Ennismore Gardens in London, or have heard Metropolitan Anthony speak about the Christian life, are conscious of a living spiritual tradition of great power and attractiveness. More than any other living Orthodox Christian, Metropolitan Anthony is for many Christians in Great Britain

11

and other Western countries the voice and face of Orthodoxy.

Many have read his books on prayer, and on our relationship with God focused in prayer: *Living Prayer*, *School for Prayer*, *Meditations on a Theme*, *Courage to Pray*, and *God and Man*. Many more could do so with great profit to their growth as Christians. The passages presented in this book exemplify the teaching, at once simple and profound, of a great Christian teacher and spiritual guide of our own time, through whom the riches of the Orthodox tradition are being made available to Christians of other traditions.

His life

Metropolitan Anthony was born on 19 June 1914 in Switzerland, where his father was serving as a member of the Russian Imperial Diplomatic Corps. His mother was the sister of the Russian composer Alexander Scriabin. Just before the First World War the family returned to Russia, but soon left again to go to Persia. After the Russian Revolution of 1917 they were obliged to leave Persia, and it was only after several unsettled years on the move that the family finally made its home in Paris in 1923. There Metropolitan Anthony completed his schooling – begun in Austria – reading classics. He went on to study physics, chemistry and biology at the Sorbonne School of Science. After graduating he studied medicine, and in 1939 qualified as a doctor.

Meanwhile he had become a Christian. In the course of the nineteenth century Orthodoxy had largely lost its hold on the educated classes in Russia. A religious renaissance had begun among the intelligentsia in the early part of the present century, only to be cut off in Russia itself by the Bolshevik Revolution. Metropolitan Anthony, like many of his contemporaries, grew up with no belief at all in God, and fiercely hostile to the Church. When he was eleven, he was sent to a boys' summer camp where he met a young priest. He was impressed by what he later described as the man's unconditional ability to love, and reckons this his first deep spiritual experience. But at the time it did nothing to shake his atheist convictions. They were undermined, however, a few years later by his first experience of perfect happiness. That came to him when, after years of hardship and struggle, his family was settled under one roof for the first time since the Revolution. But it was aimless happiness, and he found it unbearable. He was driven to look for a meaning to life. So deeply was he affected by this experience that he made up his mind to commit suicide if within a year he could find no meaning to his life.

After some months of fruitless search he was urged to support a Russian youth organization, to which he belonged, by going to a meeting at which a priest had been invited to speak. He went reluctantly, firmly intending to pay no attention. But in spite of himself he listened, becoming more and more indignant at the vision of Christ and Christianity which he found deeply repulsive. When he arrived home, he borrowed a book of the Gospels, in order to check what the speaker had said. Unwilling to waste too much time on such a profitless exercise, he chose to read St Mark's as the shortest of the Gospels. What happened then is best told in his own words:

> While I was reading the beginning of St Mark's Gospel, before I reached the third chapter, I suddenly became aware that on the other side of my desk there was a presence. And the certainty was so strong that it was Christ standing there that it has never left me. This was the real turning-point. Because Christ was alive and I had been in his presence I could say with certainty that what the Gospel said about the crucifixion of the prophet of Galilee was true, and the centurion was right when he said, 'Truly he is the Son of God'. It was in the light of the resurrection that I could read with certainty the story of the Gospel, knowing that everything was true in it because the impossible event of the resurrection was to me more certain than any other event of history. History I had to believe, the resurrection I knew for a fact. I did not discover, as you see, the Gospel beginning with its first message of the annunciation, and it did not unfold for me as a story which one can believe or disbelieve. It began as an event that left all problems of disbelief behind because it was a direct and personal experience.

During the Second World War Metropolitan Anthony worked for much of the time as a surgeon in the French Army, although in the middle of the war he spent some time in the French resistance movement. In 1943 he was professed secretly as a monk, taking the monastic vows of stability, poverty, chastity and obedience. He continued to live a hidden monastic life after the war, when he became a general practitioner.

In 1948 he was ordained priest, and his monastic vows became known. The following year he was invited to become Orthodox chaplain to the Fellowship of St Alban and St Sergius. The Fellowship had been founded in 1928 by a group of Russian Orthodox and largely Anglican British Christians, to enable Anglicans and Orthodox in particular, but more widely Eastern and Western Christians in general, to meet each other, not least in prayer and worship, and so to help forward the movement towards Christian unity. It was at St Basil's House, the Fellowship's home in London, that Metropolitan Anthony began to meet Christians in Britain, and to exert a growing influence in ever-widening circles there. He has continued to play an active part in the life of the Fellowship, regularly speaking at its annual conference and at meetings in St Basil's House.

In 1950 he was appointed as parish priest to serve the Russian Orthodox congregation in London within the jurisdiction of the Moscow Patriarchate. He has remained there ever since. In 1958 he was consecrated bishop, with responsibility for Great Britain and Ireland. Given the rank of Archbishop in 1962, he was appointed Patriarchal Exarch for Western Europe in 1963, and in 1966 was made Metropolitan. His titular see is Sourozh in the Soviet Union. To his cathedral church of All Saints and the Dormition of the Mother of God Metropolitan Anthony has attracted many people, including members of other Churches, eager to experience something of the worship of the Orthodox Church, or seeking guidance in their own search for God. His influence has extended far beyond Britain and the West to his native Russia, which he has visited regularly. Every Christmas and Easter the service at All Saints, Ennismore Gardens is broadcast, and always includes an address given by the Metropolitan.

His teaching

In Metropolitan Anthony's teaching about prayer and the Christian life the Orthodox tradition is presented in a way which reflects his own intense experience of God and prayer, and his own deep understanding of human nature. He does not speak and write about 'spirituality' as a distinct aspect of Christian theology. That word, now so fashionable in Western Christianity, is not at home in Orthodoxy, which speaks rather of 'theology', meaning knowledge of – not about – God, or quite simply, and more truly, of the Christian life. When he does use it, Metropolitan Anthony insists that it can mean nothing less than the life of the Holy Spirit in us. 'Spirituality' cannot be restricted to the practice of prayer alone, for praying and living are inseparable. To pray to God is to commit oneself to obey God's commandments in daily life, and to enter into a relationship with God in the depths of one's being is to commit oneself to a loving relationship with one's neighbour.

Nevertheless our relationship with God in

prayer is fundamental to the Christian life, and prayer is an art to be acquired through disciplined practice. We must learn to pray, and Metropolitan Anthony is practical and detailed in his guidance. We must be clear, however, that in the end our prayer is not our own, but the prayer of Christ in us and in the Church, that prayer of Christ which is prayed above all in the liturgy and the other services of the Church. The prayer of Christ grows in us as we persevere in the relentless struggle to conform our whole life to the pattern of Christ's. The body, too, needs to be trained and disciplined, for we are not disembodied souls, and our bodies cannot be excluded from our praying. They must become the peaceful servants of wills brought progressively into line with God's will.

For the will is central in Christian living and praying. At the heart of both there must of course be love for God, and the source of both is always the grace of God within us. But determination to choose good and reject evil is the key to progress in both. Disciples of Jesus must be disciplined people, since it is only when we set ourselves firmly to do the will of God that God's grace finds an opening into our life. In our own interior life, in our conduct, and in our relationships with others, we must always seek to shape our thoughts and our actions in accordance with the Gospel.

Together with an insistence on the importance of the will in the Christian life goes a necessary caution against letting our prayer be affected by our mood, or by any emotional experience we may enjoy in prayer. Our feelings are unreliable guides, and our emotions are irrelevant to the goal of prayer, which is nothing less than the transformation of our being. Prayer may at times be easy, at others difficult. What matters is that at all times it should be the offering of our determination to pray.

Prayer springs from faith in God as a living reality, with whom a relationship of a not less than personal kind can be established. That living reality which is God is not distant: he is to be found within us, in the depths of our being. Growth in our relationship with God goes hand in hand, therefore, with growth in our knowledge of ourselves. Prayer is the encounter between God as he truly is, and ourselves as we really are. If we are to make progress in prayer, we must penetrate beyond our image of God to find him as he truly is, and delve beneath the superficial personalities we present to the world to discover our real selves. Neither process is easy: the Christian life demands discipline; prayer requires rigorous honesty.

Metropolitan Anthony stresses the danger involved in the encounter with the holy God, which, since we are sinners, always entails judgement. The Christian life must therefore begin with conversion and repentance. From that beginning we must go on to let the Holy Spirit within us change us, forming in us the mind of Christ. An essential aspect of Christian discipline is prayerful meditation on the Gospels, through which Christ himself confronts us and shows us those aspects of our life where conversion is still needed. Conversion is always to the way of living taught and exemplified by Jesus Christ himself. It inescapably involves taking up the cross, and learning to die with him to our sinful self, in order that the new person may be raised up to eternal life in and with God.

The need for silence is a constant emphasis in Metropolitan Anthony's teaching on prayer and the Christian life. Not only our hearts and our minds, but our bodies too, are to be trained to an alert stillness, in which we are open to God, ready to receive what he wants to give, and open to our neighbour. Prayer is far from being a stream of words spoken without pause by us to God, and too many words can stand in the way of real prayer. Simply to be, and to be still, in the presence of God, rejoicing in his presence, is an art essential to be learnt. Words, of course, are needed. They may be the words of prayers we have learnt by heart, and which are a constant stand-by at times when we find it hard to pray. They may be words which express spontaneously what we want to say at that particular time. They may, again, be the few prayerfully repeated words of the Jesus Prayer. But words are to serve, rather than dominate, prayer; and the aim of all our praying is to build up such an awareness of God's presence that prayer becomes the constant background to the whole of our life, as well as a deliberate activity at specific times.

The goal of all Christian living and praying is the vision of the glory of God, and participation through grace in the life of God himself. The way to that end lies open to us because of the incarnation, death and resurrection of the Word of God, and the indwelling of the Holy Spirit. But each of us must decide for ourself to adventure on that way, which leads to eternal life only through the suffering and death of the cross. If we determine to learn to love God and our neighbour as Jesus loved, we shall grow in our knowledge of God. Yet God remains at the same time unknowable, and, as Metropolitan Anthony reminds us in the final passage selected, 'We must be prepared to find that the last step of our relationship with God is an act of pure adoration, face to face with a mystery into which we cannot enter'.

HUGH WYBREW

Metropolitan Anthony
of
Sourozh

Real worship

Worship to me means a relationship. I used not to be a believer, then one day I discovered God and immediately he appeared to me to be the supreme value and the total meaning of life, but at the same time a person. I think that worship can mean nothing at all to someone for whom there is no object of worship. You cannot teach worship to someone who has not got a sense of the living God; you can teach him to act as if he believed, but it will not be the spontaneous attitude which is real worship.

Therefore, as a foreword to this book on prayer, what I would like to convey is my certitude in the personal reality of a God with whom a relationship can be established. Then I would ask my reader to treat God as a neighbour, as someone, and value this knowledge in the same terms in which he values a relationship with a brother or a friend. This, I think, is essential.

One of the reasons why communal worship or private prayer seems to be so dead or so conventional is that the act of worship, which takes place in the heart communing with God, is too often missing. Every expression, either verbal or in action, may help, but they are only expressions of what is essential, namely, a deep silence of communion.

God within us

The Gospel tells us that the Kingdom of God is within us first of all. If we cannot find the Kingdom of God within us, if we cannot meet God within, in the very depth of ourselves, our chances of meeting him outside ourselves are very remote. When Gagarin came back from space and made his remarkable statement that he never saw God in heaven, one of our priests in Moscow remarked, 'If you have not seen him on earth, you will never see him in heaven'.

This is also true of what I am speaking about. If we cannot find a contact with God under our own skin, as it were, then the chances are very slight that even if I meet him face to face, I will recognize him.

St John Chrysostom said, 'Find the door of your heart, you will discover it is the door of the Kingdom of God'. So it is inward that we must turn, and not outward – but inward in a very special way. I am not saying that we must become introspective. I don't mean that we must go inward in the way one does in psychoanalysis or psychology. It is not a journey into my *own* inwardness, it is a journey *through* my own self, in order to emerge from the deepest level of self into the place where he is, the point at which God and I meet.

The birth of prayer

Prayer is the search for God, encounter with God, and going beyond this encounter in communion. Thus it is an activity, a state, and also a situation; a situation both with respect to God and to the created world.

It arises from the awareness that the world in which we live is not simply two-dimensional, imprisoned in the categories of time and space, a flat world in which we meet only the surface of things, an opaque surface covering emptiness.

Prayer is born of the discovery that the world has depths; that we are not only surrounded by visible things but that we are also immersed in and penetrated by invisible things.

And this invisible world is both the presence of God, the supreme, sublime reality, and our own deepest truth.

Prayer as encounter

Encounter is central to prayer. It is the basic category of revelation, because revelation itself is an encounter with God who gives us a new vision of the world. Everything is encounter, in Scripture as in life. It is both personal and universal, unique and exemplary.

It always has two poles: encounter with God and in him with creation, and encounter with man in his depths rooted in God's creative will, straining towards fulfilment when God will be all in all.

This encounter is personal because each of us must experience it for himself, we cannot have it second-hand. It is our own, but it also has a universal significance because it goes beyond our superficial and limited ego.

This encounter is unique because for God as for one another when we truly see, each of us is irreplaceable and unique. Each creature knows God in his own way. Each one of us knows God in our own way which no one else will ever know unless we tell them. And at the same time because human nature is universal, each encounter is exemplary. It is a revelation to all of what is known personally to each.

Encounter in truth

An encounter is only true when the two persons meeting are true. And from this point of view, we are continually falsifying this encounter. Not only in ourselves but in our image of God, it is very difficult for us to be true. Throughout the day we are a succession of social personalities, sometimes unrecognizable to others or even to ourselves.

And when the time comes to pray and we want to present ourselves to God we often feel lost because we do not know which of these social personalities is the true human person, and have no sense of our own true identity. The several successive persons that we present to God are not ourselves. There is something of us in each of them but the whole person is missing.

And that is why a prayer which could rise powerfully from the heart of a true person cannot find its way between the successive men of straw we offer to God. Each of these speaks a word which is true in its own partial way, but does not express the other partial personalities we have been during the day. It is extremely important that we find our unity, our fundamental identity. Otherwise we cannot encounter the Lord in truth.

True God

The God we encounter must be as true as we who seek him. But is not God always true? Is he not always himself, unchanging? Of course.

But it is not only God as he is in himself who is involved in our prayers. It is also the image we have of him, for our attitude depends not only on what he is in himself but also on what we believe him to be.

If we have a false image of God, our attitude towards him and our prayer will alter accordingly. It is important that throughout our life, from day to day, we learn to know God as he is.

Reading Scripture (1)

When we read the Scriptures honestly we can admit that certain passages mean little to us. We are ready to agree with God because we have no reason to disagree with him. We can approve of this or that commandment or divine action because it does not touch us personally, we do not yet see the demands it makes on us personally.

Other passages frankly repel us. If we had the courage we would say 'no' to the Lord. We should note these passages carefully. They are a measure of the distance between God and us and also they are a measure of the distance between ourselves as we are now and our potential definitive selves.

For the gospel is not a succession of external commandments, it is a whole gallery of internal portraits. And every time we say 'no' to the gospel we are refusing to be a person in the full sense of the word.

Reading Scripture (2)

There are passages of the gospel which make our hearts burn, which give light to our intelligence and shake up our will. They give life and strength to our whole physical and moral being. These passages reveal the points where God and his image in us already coincide, the stage we have already reached, perhaps only momentarily, fleetingly, in becoming what we are called to be.

We should note these passages even more carefully than the passages mentioned above. They are the points at which God's image is already present in us fallen men. And from these beginnings we can strive to continue our transformation into the person we feel we want and ought to be. We must be faithful to these revelations. In this at least we must always be faithful.

If we do this these passages increase in number, the demands of the gospel become fuller and more precise, slowly the fogs disperse and we see the image of the person we should be. Then we can begin standing before God in truth.

Disciplined meditation

On many occasions we can do a lot of thinking; there are plenty of situations in our daily life in which we have nothing to do except wait, and if we are disciplined – and this is part of our spiritual training – we will be able to concentrate quickly and fix our attention at once on the subject of our thoughts, of our meditation. We must learn to do it by compelling our thoughts to attach themselves to one focus and to drop everything else.

In the beginning, extraneous thoughts will intrude, but if we push them away constantly, time after time, in the end they will leave us in peace. It is only when by training, by exercise, by habit, we have become able to concentrate profoundly and quickly, that we can continue through life in a state of collectedness, in spite of what we are doing.

Method of meditation

Often we consider one or two points and jump to the next, which is wrong since we have just seen that it takes a long time to become recollected, what the Fathers call an attentive person, someone capable of paying attention to an idea so long and so well that nothing of it is lost.

The spiritual writers of the past and of the present day will all tell us: take a text, ponder on it hour after hour, day after day, until you have exhausted all your possibilities, intellectual and emotional, and thanks to attentive reading and re-reading of this text, you have come to a new attitude.

Quite often meditation consists in nothing but examining the text, turning over these words of God addressed to us so as to become completely familiar with them, so imbued with them that gradually we and these words become completely one. In this process, even if we think we have not found any particular intellectual richness, we have changed.

Prayer and meditation contrasted

Meditation is an activity of thought, while prayer is the rejection of every thought. According to the teaching of the Eastern Fathers, even pious thoughts and the deepest and loftiest theological considerations, if they occur during prayer, must be considered as a temptation and suppressed; because, as the Fathers say, it is foolish to think about God and forget that you are in his presence.

All the spiritual guides of Orthodoxy warn us against replacing this meeting with God by thinking about him. Prayer is essentially standing face to face with God, consciously striving to remain collected and absolutely still and attentive in his presence, which means standing with an undivided mind, an undivided heart and an undivided will in the presence of the Lord; and that is not easy.

Whatever our training may give us, there is always a short-cut open at any time: undividedness can be attained by the person for whom the love of God is everything, who has broken all ties, who is completely given to God; then there is no longer personal striving, but the working of the radiant grace of God.

The purpose of meditation

The purpose of meditation is not to achieve an academic exercise in thinking; it is not meant to be a purely intellectual performance, nor a beautiful piece of thinking without further consequences; it is meant to be a piece of straight thinking under God's guidance and Godwards, and should lead us to draw conclusions about how to live. It is important to realize from the outset that a meditation has been useful when, as a result, it enables us to live more precisely and more concretely in accordance with the gospel.

Whatever we take, a verse, a commandment, an event in the life of Christ, we must first of all assess its real objective content. This is extremely important because the purpose of meditation is not to build up a fantastic structure but to understand a truth.

The truth is there, it is God's truth, and meditation is meant to be a bridge between our lack of understanding and the truth revealed. It is a way in which we can educate our intelligence, and gradually learn to have 'the mind of Christ', as St Paul says (1 Co 2:16).

Creative living

The day itself is blessed by God. Doesn't this mean that everything that it contains, everything that happens to us during it is within the will of God? Believing that things happen merely by chance is not believing in God. And if we receive everything that happens and everyone who comes to us in this spirit, we shall see that we are called to do the work of Christians in everything.

Every encounter is an encounter in God and in his sight. We are sent to everyone we meet on our way, either to give or to receive, sometimes without even knowing it. Sometimes we experience the wonder of giving what we did not possess, sometimes we have to pay with our own blood for what we give.

We must also know how to receive. We must be able to encounter our neighbour, to look at him, hear him, keep silence, pay attention, be able to love and to respond wholeheartedly to what is offered, whether it be bitterness or joy, sad or wonderful. We should be completely open and like putty in God's hands. The things that happen in our life, accepted as God's gifts, will thus give us the opportunity to be continually creative, doing the work of a Christian.

Shallow depths

If you watch your life carefully you will discover quite soon that we hardly ever live from within outwards; instead we respond to incitement, to excitement. In other words, we live by reflection, by reaction. Something happens and we respond, someone speaks and we answer.

But when we are left without anything that stimulates us to think, speak or act, we realize that there is very little in us that will prompt us to action in any direction at all.

This is really a very dramatic discovery. We are completely empty, we do not act from within ourselves but accept as our life a life which is actually fed in from outside; we are used to things happening which compel us to do other things. How seldom can we live simply by means of the depth and the richness we assume that there is within ourselves.

The start of prayer

What we must start with, if we wish to pray, is the certainty that we are sinners in need of salvation, that we are cut off from God and that we cannot live without him and that all we can offer God is our desperate longing to be made such that God will receive us, receive us in repentance, receive us with mercy and with love.

And so from the outset prayer is really our humble ascent towards God, a moment when we turn Godwards, shy of coming near, knowing that if we meet him too soon, before his grace has had time to help us to be capable of meeting him, it will be judgement.

And all we can do is to turn to him with all the reverence, all the veneration, the worshipful adoration, the fear of God of which we are capable, with all the attention and earnestness which we may possess, and ask him to do something with us that will make us capable of meeting him face to face, not for judgement, nor for condemnation, but for eternal life.

The condition for a life of prayer

I should like to stress that encounter with God and man is dangerous. It is not without reason that the Eastern tradition of Zen calls the place where we find him whom we seek the tiger's lair. Seeking God is an act of boldness, unless it is an act of complete humility. Encountering God is always a crisis and the Greek word crisis means judgement. This encounter can take place in wonder and humility. It can also take place in terror and condemnation.

So it is not surprising that Orthodox manuals on prayer give very little space to questions of technique and method but endless advice on the necessary moral and spiritual conditions for prayer. Let us recall first the gospel commandment (Mt 5:23–24): 'If you come to the temple and you remember your brother has something against you, leave your gift, return to him you have offended and make your peace with him, then come back and offer your gift.'

This commandment is taken up in an excellent manner by Simeon the New Theologian, who tells us that if we want to pray with a free heart, we must make our peace with God, our conscience, our neighbour, and even the things about us. That is to say that the condition of a life of prayer is a life in accordance with the gospel. A life which makes the commandments and counsels given us by the gospel second nature.

Conversion

We see that we cannot partake deeply of the life of God unless we change profoundly. It is therefore essential that we should go to God in order that he should transform and change us, and that is why, to begin with, we should ask for conversion. Conversion in Latin means a turn, a change in the direction of things. The Greek word *metanoia* means a change of mind.

Conversion means that instead of spending our lives in looking in all directions, we should follow one direction only. It is a turning away from a great many things which we value solely because they were pleasant or expedient for us. The first impact of conversion is to modify our sense of values: God being at the centre of all, everything acquires a new position and a new depth. All that is God's, all that belongs to him, is positive and real. Everything that is outside him has no value or meaning.

But it is not a change of mind alone that we can call conversion. We can change our minds and go no farther; what must follow is an act of will and unless our will comes into motion and is redirected Godwards, there is no conversion; at most there is only an incipient, still dormant and inactive change in us.

Repentance

Repentance must not be mistaken for remorse, it does not consist in feeling terribly sorry that things went wrong in the past; it is an active, positive attitude which consists in moving in the right direction.

It is made very clear in the parable of the two sons (Mt 21:28) who were commanded by their father to go to work at his vineyard. The one said, 'I am going', but did not go. The other said, 'I am not going', and then felt ashamed and went to work.

This was real repentance, and we should never lure ourselves into imagining that to lament one's past is an act of repentance. It is part of it, of course, but repentance remains unreal and barren as long as it has not led us to doing the will of the Father. We have a tendency to think that it should result in fine emotions and we are quite often satisfied with emotions instead of real, deep changes.

The known and unknown God

We may have understood a great deal about God from our own experience, from the experience of others, from the writings of the saints, from the teaching of the Church, from the witness of the Scriptures; we may know that he is good, that he is humble, that he is a burning fire, that he is our judge, that he is our saviour and a great many other things, but we must remember that he may at any time reveal himself in a way in which we have never perceived him, even within these general categories.

We must take our stand before him with reverence and be ready to meet whomever we shall meet, either the God who is already familiar or a God we cannot recognize. He may give us a sense of what he is and it may be quite different from what we expect. We hope to meet Jesus, mild, compassionate, loving, and we meet God who judges and condemns and will not let us come near in our present state. Or we come in repentance, expecting to be rejected, and we meet compassion.

God, at every stage, is for us partly known and partly unknown. He reveals himself, and thus far we know him, but we shall never know him completely, there will always be the divine mystery, a core of mystery which we shall never be able to penetrate.

God's silence

The encounter between God and us in stable prayer always leads to silence. We have to learn to distinguish two sorts of silence: God's silence and our own inner silence. First, the silence of God, often harder to bear than his refusal, the absent silence we spoke of earlier. Second, the silence of man, deeper than speech, in closer communion with God than any words.

God's silence to our prayer can last only a short time or it may seem to go on for ever. Christ was silent to the prayers of the Canaanite woman and this led her to gather up all her faith and hope and human love to offer to God so that he might extend the conditions of his Kingdom beyond the chosen people. The silence of Christ provoked her to respond, to grow in her capacity.

And God may do the same to us with shorter or longer silences to summon our strength and faithfulness and lead us to a deeper relationship with him than would have been possible had it been easy. But sometimes the silence seems frighteningly final to us.

Man's silence

God's silence and absence, but also man's silence and absence. An encounter does not become deep and full until the two parties to it are capable of being silent with one another. As long as we need words and actions, tangible proof, this means we have not reached the depth and fullness we seek. We have not experienced the silence which enfolds two people in common intimacy. It goes deep down, deeper than we knew we were, an inner silence where we encounter God, and with God and in God our neighbour.

In this state of silence we do not need words to feel close to our companion, to communicate with him in our deepest being, beyond ourselves to something which unites us. And when the silence is deep enough, we can begin to speak from its depths, but carefully and cautiously so as not to break it by the noisy disorder of our words. Then our thought is contemplative.

Our mind, instead of trying to make distinctions between many forms, as it usually does, tries to elicit simple luminous forms from the depths of the heart. The mind does its true work. It serves him who expresses something greater than it. We look into depths beyond ourselves and try to express something of what we find with awe and reverence. Such words, if they do not trivialize or intellectualize the total experience, do not break the silence, but express it.

God the sole focus of attention

God must always be the focus of our attention, for there are many ways in which this collectedness may be falsified; when we pray from a deep concern, we have a sense that our whole being has become one prayer and we imagine that we have been in a state of deep, real, prayerful collectedness, but this is not true, because the focus of attention was not God; it was the object of our prayer.

When we are emotionally involved, no alien thought intrudes, because we are completely concerned with what we are praying about; it is only when we turn to pray for some other person or need that our attention is suddenly dispersed, which means that it was not the thought of God, not the sense of his presence that was the cause of this concentration, but our human concern.

It does not mean that human concern is of no importance, but it means that the thought of a friend can do more than the thought of God, which is a serious point.

Praying within the Kingdom

In order to be able to pray, we must be within the situation which is defined as the Kingdom of God. We must recognize that he is God, that he is King, we must surrender to him. We must at least be concerned with his will, even if we are not yet capable of fulfilling it.

But if we are not, if we treat God like the rich young man who could not follow Christ because he was too rich, then how can we meet him? So often what we would like to have through prayer, through the deep relationship with God which we long for, is simply another period of happiness; we are not prepared to sell all that we have in order to buy the pearl of great price.

Then how should we get this pearl of great price? Is that what we expect to get? Is it not the same as in human relationships: when a man or a woman experiences love for another, other people no longer matter in the same way. To put it in a short formula from the ancient world, 'When a man has a bride, he is no longer surrounded by men and women, but by people'. Isn't that what could, what should happen with regard to all our riches when we turn to God?

Putting God first

Love and friendship do not grow if we are not prepared to sacrifice a great deal for their sake, and in the same way we must be ready to put aside many things in order to give God the first place.

'Thou shalt love the Lord thy God with all thy heart, and with all thy soul, and with all thy strength, and with all thy mind' (Lk 10:27). This seems to be a very simple command, and yet those words contain much more than one sees at a first glance. We all know what it is to love someone with all one's heart; we know the pleasure, not only of meeting but even of thinking of the beloved, the warm comfort it gives. it is in that way that we should try to love God, and whenever his name is mentioned, it should fill our heart and soul with infinite warmth. God should be at all times in our mind, whereas in fact we think of him only occasionally.

As for loving God with all our strength, we can only do it if we cast off deliberately everything that is not God's in us; by an effort of will we must turn ourselves constantly towards God, whether in prayer, which is easier, because in prayer we are already centred on God, or in action, which requires training, because in our actions we are concentrated on some material achievement and have to dedicate it to God by a special effort.

The mystery of being

Whatever we do, however well we know him, however close we are, and this is even truer of man and God than man and man, there remains a central mystery which we can never solve. In the Book of Revelation there is a marvellous passage where John says that those who go into the Kingdom are given a white stone with a name written on it which only they and God know.

This name is not the label we are given and called by in this world. Our true name, our eternal name exactly fits us, our whole being . . . It defines and expresses us perfectly. It is known by God alone and he tells us what it is. No one else can know it because it expresses our unique relationship with our Creator.

How often human relationships come to grief because one person wants to reveal himself beyond what is possible or the other person wants to probe into a territory which is sacred to God alone. It is a vain wish and cannot be fulfilled. It is like a child trying to find the source of a spring, the point where the water begins, that point just before there is no water. In this case it is only possible to destroy, not to discover.

Meaningful prayer

Unless the prayer which you intend to offer to God is important and meaningful to you first, you will not be able to present it to the Lord. If you are inattentive to the words you pronounce, if your heart does not respond to them, or if your life is not turned in the same direction as your prayer, it will not reach out Godwards.

So the first thing is to choose a prayer which you can say with all your mind, with all your heart and with all your will – a prayer which does not necessarily have to be a great example of liturgical art, but which must be true, something which should not fall short of what you want to express. You must understand this prayer, with all the richness and precision it possesses.

You must also put all the heart you can into an act of worship, an act of recognition of God, an act of cherishing, which is the true meaning of charity, an action which involves you in the mind, in the heart, and an action which is completely adequate to what you are.

Unmoved by moods

When we are in the right frame of mind, when the heart is full of worship, of concern for others, when, as St Luke says, our lips speak from the fullness of the heart (6:45), there is no problem about praying; we speak freely to God in the words that are most familiar to us.

But if we were to leave our life of prayer at the mercy of our moods, we should probably pray from time to time fervently and sincerely, but lose for long periods any prayerful contact with God. It is a great temptation to put off praying till the moment when we feel alive to God, and to consider that any prayer or move Godwards at other periods lacks sincerity. We all know from experience that we have a variety of feelings which do not come to the fore at every moment of our lives; illness or distress can blot them from our consciousness. Even when we love deeply, there are times when we are not aware of it and yet we know that love is alive in us.

The same is true with regard to God; there are inner and outward causes that make it difficult at times to be aware of the fact that we believe, that we have hope, that we do love God. At such moments we must act not on the strength of what we feel but of what we know.

The irrelevance of emotions

In our struggle for prayer the emotions are almost irrelevant; what we must bring to God is a complete, firm determination to be faithful to him and strive that God should live in us. We must remember that the fruits of prayer are not this or that emotional state, but a deep change in the whole of our personality.

What we aim at is to be made able to stand before God and to concentrate on his presence, all our needs being directed Godwards, and to be given power, strength, anything we need that the will of God may be fulfilled in us. That the will of God should be fulfilled in us is the only aim of prayer, and it is also the criterion of right prayer. It is not the mystical feeling we may have, or our emotions that make good praying.

Theophane the Recluse says: 'You ask yourself, "Have I prayed well today?" Do not try to find out how deep your emotions were, or how much deeper you understand things divine; ask yourself: "Am I doing God's will better than I did before?" If you are, prayer has brought its fruits, if you are not, it has not, whatever amount of understanding or feeling you may have derived from the time spent in the presence of God.'

Will in the Christian life

Concentration, whether in meditation or in prayer, can only be achieved by an effort of will. Our spiritual life is based on our faith and determination, and any incidental joys are a gift of God. St Seraphim of Sarov, when asked what it was that made some people remain sinners and never make any progress while others were becoming saints and living in God, answered: 'Only determination'.

Our activities must be determined by an act of will, which usually happens to be contrary to what we long for; this will, based on our faith, always clashes with another will, our instinctive one. There are two wills in us, one is the conscious will, possessed to a greater or lesser degree, which consists in the ability to compel ourselves to act in accordance with our convictions. The second one is something else in us. It is the longings, the claims, the desires of all our nature, quite often contrary to the first will.

St Paul speaks of the two laws that fight against each other (Rm 7:23). He speaks of the old and new Adam in us, who are at war. It is not enough to aim at the victory of the good will against the evil one; the evil one, that is the longings of our fallen nature, must absolutely, though gradually, be transformed into a longing, a craving, for God. The struggle is hard and far-reaching.

Disciplined discipleship

Doing the will of God is a discipline in the best sense of the word. It is also a test of our loyalty, of our fidelity to Christ. It is by doing in every detail, at every moment, to the utmost of our power, as perfectly as we can, with the greatest moral integrity, using our intelligence, our imagination, our will, our skill, our experience, that we can gradually learn to be strictly, earnestly obedient to the Lord God.

Unless we do this our discipleship is an illusion and all our life of discipline, when it is a set of self-imposed rules in which we delight, which makes us proud and self-satisfied, leaves us nowhere, because the essential momentum of our discipleship is the ability to reject our self, to allow the Lord Christ to be our mind, our will and our heart. Unless we renounce ourselves and accept his life in place of our life, unless we aim at what St Paul defines as 'it is no longer I but Christ who lives in me', we shall never be either disciplined or disciples.

Discipline and grace

Spiritual discipline is a road, a way in which we open ourselves to Christ, to the grace of God. This is all discipline, all we can do. It is God who in response to this ascetical endeavour will give us his grace and fulfil us.

We have a tendency to think that what we are to aim at is a high, deep, mystical life. This is not what we should aim at. A mystical life is a gift from God; in itself it is not an achievement of ours and even less is it an expression of our devotion to God.

What we must aim at in response to the love of God declared, manifest in Christ, is to become true disciples by bringing ourselves as a sacrifice to God; on our part it is the ascetical endeavour which is the summit of our loyalty, allegiance and love. We must offer this to God and he will fulfil all things as he has promised. 'My child, give me thy heart; I shall fulfil all things.'

Prayer and life

As long as we care deeply for all the trivialities of life, we cannot hope to pray wholeheartedly; they will always colour the train of our thoughts. The same is true about our daily relations with other people, which should not consist merely of gossip but be based on what is essential in every one of us, otherwise we may find ourselves unable to reach another level when we turn to God.

We must eradicate everything meaningless and trivial in ourselves and in our relations with others, and concentrate on those things we shall be able to take with us into eternity.

It is not possible to become another person the moment we start to pray, but by keeping watch on one's thoughts one learns gradually to differentiate their value. It is in our daily life that we cultivate the thoughts which irrepressibly spring up at the time of prayer. Prayer in its turn will change and enrich our daily life, becoming the foundation of a new and real relationship with God and those around us.

Prayer and commitment

Words of prayer have the quality of always being words of commitment. You cannot simply say words of prayer without implying 'If I say that, then that is what I am going to do when the occasion lends itself'. When you say to God, 'At all costs, at all costs, O Lord, save me', you must remember that you must put all your will into that, because one day God will say, 'Here is the price to pay'.

The ancient writers said, 'Give your blood and God will give you the Spirit'. That is the price. Abandon all, you will receive heaven; abandon enslavement, you will acquire freedom. As your will is already engaged not only in the act of praying but in all the consequences of this prayer, so also must your body be, because a human being is not simply a soul engaged for a while in a body. It is a being which is body and soul, one unique being which is Man.

There is a physical effort to be made in prayer, the physical attention, the physical way in which you pray. Fasting, if food has made you too heavy for prayer, is involved in it too. If you do this, you will be knocking at a door.

Christian prayer

The characteristic of Christian prayer is that it is the prayer of Christ, brought to his Father, from generation to generation in constantly renewed situations, by those who, by grace and participation, are Christ's presence in this world; it is a continuous, unceasing prayer to God, that God's will should be done, that all should happen according to his wise and loving plan.

This means that our life of prayer is at the same time a struggle against all that is not Christ's. We prepare the ground for our prayer each time we shed something which is not Christ's, which is unworthy of him, and only the prayer of one who can, like St Paul, say: 'I live, yet not I, but Christ liveth in me' (Ga 2:20) is real Christian prayer.

Your will be done

As the Church is an extension of Christ's presence in time and space, any Christian prayer should be Christ praying, although it implies a purity of heart we do not possess. The prayers of the Church are Christ's prayers, particularly in the canon of the liturgy, where it is entirely Christ praying; but any other prayer in which we ask for something involving a concrete situation is always under 'if'.

In the majority of cases we do not know what Christ would have prayed for in this situation and so we introduce the 'if', which means that as far as we can see, as far as we know God's will, this is what we wish to happen to meet his will.

But the 'if' also means: I am putting into these words my desire that the best should happen, and therefore you can alter this concrete petition to anything you choose, taking my intention, the desire that your will be done, even if I am unwise in stating how I should like it to be done (Rm 8:26).

The silence of discipleship

Discipleship begins with silence and listening. When we listen to someone, we think we are silent because we do not speak; but our minds continue to work, our emotions react, our will responds for or against what we hear, we may even go further than this, with thoughts and feelings buzzing in our heads which are quite unrelated to what is being said. This is not silence as it is implied in discipleship.

The real silence towards which we must aim as a starting-point is a complete repose of mind and heart and will, the complete silence of all there is in us, including our body, so that we may be completely aware of the word we are receiving, completely alert and yet in complete repose.

The silence I am speaking of is the silence of the sentry on duty at a critical moment; alert, immobile, poised and yet alive to every sound, every movement. This living silence is what discipleship requires first of all, and this is not achieved without effort. It requires from us a training of our attention, a training of our body, a training of our mind and our emotions so that they are kept in check, completely and perfectly.

A peaceful body

We must learn to acquire a peaceful body. Whatever our psychological activity, our body reacts to it; and our bodily state determines to a certain degree the type or quality of our psychological activity.

Theophane the Recluse, in his advice to anyone wishing to attempt the spiritual life, says that one of the conditions indispensable to success is never to permit bodily slackness: 'Be like a violin string, tuned to a precise note, without slackness or supertension, the body erect, shoulders back, carriage of the head easy, the tensions of all muscles orientated towards the heart.'

A great deal has been written and said about the ways in which one can make use of the body to increase one's ability to be attentive, but on a level accessible to many, Theophane's advice seems to be simple, precise and practical. We must learn to relax and be alert at the same time. We must master our body so that it should not intrude but make collectedness easier for us.

Unworthy prayer purified

Sometimes we think that we are unworthy of praying and that we even have no right to pray. This is a temptation. Every drop of water, from wherever it comes, pool or ocean, is purified in the process of evaporation; and so is every prayer ascending to God.

The more dejected we feel, the greater the necessity for prayer. This is surely what John of Kronstadt felt one day when he was praying, watched by a devil who was muttering, 'You hypocrite, how dare you pray with your filthy mind, full of the thoughts I read in it'. He answered, 'It is just because my mind is full of thoughts I dislike and fight that I am praying to God'.

Spontaneous prayer

Spontaneous prayer is possible in two situations: either at moments when we have become vividly aware of God, when this awareness calls out of us a response of worship, of joy, all the forms of response we are capable of giving, being ourselves and facing the living God, or when we become aware suddenly of the deathly danger in which we are when we come to God, moments when we suddenly shout out from the depths of despair and dereliction, and also from the sense that there is no hope of salvation for us unless God saves us.

Spontaneous prayer must gush out of our souls, we cannot simply turn on a tap and get it out. It is not there for us to draw from to use at any moment. It comes from the depths of our soul, from either wonder or distress, but it does not come from the middle situation in which we are neither overwhelmed by the divine presence nor overwhelmed by a sense of who we are and the position in which we are. So that, at those moments, to try to use a spontaneous prayer is a completely illusory exercise.

Prayer of conviction

There is need for some sort of prayer which is not spontaneous but which is truly rooted in conviction. To find this you can draw from a great many of the existing prayers. We already have a rich panoply of prayers which were wrought in the throes of faith, by the Holy Spirit.

For example, we have the Psalms, we have so many short and long prayers in the liturgical wealth of all the Churches from which we can draw. What matters is that you should learn and know enough of such prayers so that at the right moment you are able to find the right prayers. It is a question of learning by heart enough meaningful passages, from the Psalms or from the prayers of the saints.

Learn those passages, because one day when you are so completely low, so profoundly desperate that you cannot call out of your soul any spontaneous expression, any spontaneous wording, you will discover that these words come up and offer themselves to you as a gift of God, as a gift of the Church, as a gift of holiness, helping our simple lack of strength. And then you really need the prayers you have learnt and made a part of yourself.

Continuous prayer

A last way in which we can pray is the use, more or less continuous, of a vocal prayer that serves as a background, a walking-stick, throughout the day and throughout life.

What I have in mind is something which is specifically used by the Orthodox. It is what we call the 'Jesus Prayer', a prayer which is centred on the name of Jesus. 'Lord Jesus Christ, son of God, have mercy on me a sinner.' This prayer is used by monks and nuns but also it is used by our lay people.

It is the prayer of stability, because it is the prayer that is not discursive – we do not move from one thought to another – it is a prayer that places us face to face with God through a profession of faith concerning him, and it defines a situation concerning us. It is the profession of faith which, according to the mind of most Orthodox ascetics and mystics, is a summing up of the whole Gospels.

Constant prayer

It is difficult to pray for a whole day. Sometimes we try and imagine what it would be like. We think either of the liturgical life of contemplative monks or else the anchorite's life of prayer. We don't so often think of a life of prayer taking place in ordinary life, when everything becomes prayer or an occasion for prayer. But this is an easy way to pray, although it is of course very demanding.

Let us rise in the morning and offer ourselves to God. We have woken from a sleep which divides us from yesterday. Waking up offers us a new reality, a day which has never existed before, an unknown time and space stretching before us like a field of untrodden snow. Let us ask the Lord to bless this day and bless us in it.

And when we have done this, let us take our request seriously and also the silent answer we have been given. We are blessed by God, his blessing will be with us always in everything we do which is capable of receiving this blessing. We will only lose it when we turn away from God. And God will stay near us even then, ready to come to our aid, ready to give us back the grace we have rejected.

Petition

Many of our prayers are prayers of petition, and people seem to think that petition is the lowest level of prayer; then comes gratitude, then praise.

But in fact it is gratitude and praise that are expressions of a lower relationship. On our level of half-belief it is easier to sing hymns of praise or to thank God than to trust him enough to ask something with faith. Even people who believe half-heartedly can turn to thank God when something nice comes their way; and there are moments of elation when everyone can sing to God.

But it is much more difficult to have such undivided faith as to ask with one's whole heart and whole mind with complete confidence. No one should look askance at petition, because the ability to say prayers of petition is a test of the reality of our faith.

Knitting before God

I remember that one of the first people who came to me for advice when I was ordained was an old lady who said: 'Father, I have been praying almost unceasingly for fourteen years, and I have never had any sense of God's presence.' So I said: 'Did you give him a chance to put in a word?' 'Oh well', she said, 'no, I have been talking to him all this time, because is not that prayer?' I said: 'No, I do not think it is, and what I suggest is that you should set apart fifteen minutes a day, sit and just knit before the face of God.'

And so she did. What was the result? Quite soon she came again and said: 'It is extraordinary, when I pray to God, in other words when I talk to him, I feel nothing, but when I sit quietly, face to face with him, then I feel wrapped in his presence.'

You will never be able to pray to God really and from all your heart unless you learn to keep silent and rejoice in the miracle of his presence, or if you prefer, of your being face to face with him although you do not see him.

Sense of the presence of God

If you learn to use a prayer you have chosen at moments when you can give all your attention to the divine presence and offer God this prayer, gradually what happens is that the awareness of God grows within you to such an extent that whether you are with people, listening, speaking or whether you are alone working, this awareness is so strong that even if you are with people you will still be able to pray.

When a great joy has come upon us or a great pain or a great sorrow, we do not forget it in the course of the day. We listen to people, we do our work, we read, we do what we are supposed to, and the pain of bereavement, the awareness of joy, of the exhilarating news is with us incessantly. This should also be the sense of the presence of God.

And if the sense of the presence of God is as clear as that, then one can pray while one does other things. One can pray while one works physically, but one can also pray when one is with people, listening or being engaged in some sort of conversation or relationship. But this is not the first thing that happens to us, and we must school ourselves to an attitude of worshipful attention and of broken-heartedness first, in those conditions which allow it, because it is easy to get inattentive, to slip from alertness to dreaming in prayer.

Contemplation and intercession

The fact that we are present in a situation alters it profoundly because God is then present with us through our faith. Wherever we are, at home with our family, with friends when a quarrel is about to begin, at work or even simply in the Underground, the street, the train, we can recollect ourselves and say, 'Lord, I believe in you, come and be among us'.

And by this act of faith, in a contemplative prayer which does not ask to see, we can intercede with God who has promised his presence when we ask for it. Sometimes we have no words, sometimes we do not know how to act wisely, but we can always ask God to come and be present. And we shall see how often the atmosphere changes, quarrels stop, peace comes.

This is not a minor mode of intercession, although it is less spectacular than a great sacrifice. We see in it again how contemplation and action are inseparable, that Christian action is impossible without contemplation. We see also how such contemplation is not a vision of God alone, but a deep vision of everything enabling us to see its eternal meaning. Contemplation is a vision not of God alone, but of the world in God.

Unanswered prayer

'Ask and it shall be given' (Mt 7:7). These words are a thorn in the Christian consciousness, they can be neither accepted nor rejected. To reject them would mean a refusal of God's infinite kindness, but we are not yet Christian enough to accept them.

We know that the Father would not give a stone instead of bread (Mt 7:9), but we do not think of ourselves as children who are unconscious of their real needs and what is good or bad for them. Yet there lies the explanation of so many unanswered prayers.

It can also be found in the words of St John Chrysostom: 'Do not be distressed if you do not receive at once what you ask for: God wants to do you more good through your perseverance in prayer.'

Prayer of perfect silence

There are times when we do not need any words of prayer, neither our own nor anyone else's and then we pray in perfect silence. This perfect silence is the ideal prayer, provided, however, that the silence is real and not daydreaming.

We have very little experience of what deep silence of body and soul means, when complete serenity fills the soul, when complete peace fills the body, when there is no turmoil or stirring of any sort and when we stand before God, completely open in an act of adoration. There may be times when we feel physically well and mentally relaxed, tired of words because we have used so many of them already; we do not want to stir and we feel happy in this fragile balance; this is on the borderline of slipping into daydreaming.

Inner silence is absence of any sort of inward stirring of thought or emotion, but it is complete alertness, openness to God. We must keep silence when we can, but never allow it to degenerate into simple contentment. To prevent this the great writers of Orthodoxy warn us never to abandon completely the normal forms of prayer, because even those who have reached this contemplative silence found it necessary, whenever they were in danger of spiritual slackness, to reintroduce words of prayer until prayer had renewed silence.

The communion of saints and sinners

The Church makes no distinction between the living and the dead. God is not the God of the dead, he is the God of the living. For him all men are alive, and so they are for the Church.

Within this eschatological perspective we can see death as the great hope and joyfully await the judgement and the coming of Christ. We can say with the Spirit of the Church, 'Come soon, Lord Jesus'. History and eternity are one, eschatologically and eucharistically.

The prayer of the Church includes not only the members of the Church but through them and because of them the whole world. She sees the whole world as the potential Church, the total Church for which she hopes. And in the Church, within this eschatology, all things are already accomplished as well as being in process. We have a living relationship in the communion of saints and sinners with all the living and the dead.

Prayer for the dead

If you believe that prayers for the living are a help to them, why should you not pray for the dead? Life is one, for as St Luke says: 'He is not the God of the dead but of the living' (20:38). Death is not an end but a stage in the destiny of man, and this destiny is not petrified at the moment of death.

The love which our prayer expresses cannot be in vain; if love had power on earth and had no power after death it would tragically contradict the word of Scripture that love is as strong as death (Sg 8:6), and the experience of the Church that love is more powerful than death, because Christ has defeated death in his love for mankind.

Prayer to the dead

We pray not only for certain people but to certain people. We pray to Mary and the saints. But we do not pray to them to turn away God's strict justice by their gentleness. We know that their will and God's are one and this harmony includes in charity all the living and the dead. If it is true that our God is not the God of the dead but of the living, isn't it natural that we should pray to those who are particularly shining examples for us?

We can each find among the saints one that particularly attracts us. We do not make a radical distinction between those who are saints and those who are not. Certain saints were set apart by God as examples for all Christians. This does not mean that others were not. And it is quite proper for us to pray to our dead parents and friends without this being blasphemy.

True humility

Humility does not consist in forever trying to abase ourselves and renounce the dignity which God gives us and demands of us because we are his children not his slaves. Humility as we see it in the saints is not born solely of their awareness of sin, because even a sinner can bring to God a broken and contrite heart and a word of forgiveness is enough to blot out all evil from the past and the present.

The humility of the saints comes from the vision of the glory, the majesty, the beauty of God. It is not even a sense of contrast that gives birth to their humility, but the consciousness that God is so holy, such a revelation of perfect beauty, of love so striking that the only thing they can do in his presence is to prostrate themselves before him in an act of worship, joy and wonder.

When the great experience of the overwhelming love that God has for us came to St Teresa, she was struck to her knees, weeping in joy and wonder; when she arose she was a new person, one in whom the realization of God's love left her 'with a sense of unpayable debt'. This is humility – not humiliation.

Holiness

It is very important for the comprehension of holiness to understand that it has two poles: *God* and the *world*. Its source, its fulcrum and its content is God; but its point of impact, the place into which it is born, where it develops and also where it is expressed in terms of Christ's salvation, is the world, this ambiguous world which, on the one hand, was created by God and is the object of such love that the Father gave his only-begotten Son for its salvation, and on the other hand, has fallen into the slavery of evil.

This pole of holiness which relates to the world therefore has two aspects: a vision of the world as God willed it, as he loves it, and at the same time an asceticism which requires us to disengage ourselves from the world and free the world from the grip of Satan.

This second element, this battle which is our vocation, is part and parcel of holiness. The Desert Fathers, the ascetics of early times, did not flee from the world in the sense in which modern man sometimes tries to escape its grip in order to find a haven of security; they set out to conquer the Enemy in battle. By the grace of God, in the power of the Spirit, they were engaging in combat.

God's holiness in us

All holiness is God's holiness in us: it is a holiness that is participation and, in a certain way, more than participation, because as we participate in what we can receive from God, we become a revelation of that which transcends us. Being a limited light, we reveal the light.

But we should also remember that in this life in which we are striving towards holiness, our spirituality should be defined in very objective and precise terms. When we read books on spirituality or engage in studying the subject, we see that spirituality, explicitly or implicitly, is repeated defined as an attitude, a state of soul, an inner condition, a type of interiority, and so on.

In reality, if you look for the ultimate definition and try to discover the inner core of spirituality, you find that spirituality does not consist in the states of soul that are familiar to us, but that it is the presence and action of the Holy Spirit in us, by us and through us in the world. There is no other holiness than that of God; it is as the Body of Christ that we can participate in holiness, in Christ and in the Holy Spirit.

The church as sacred ground

When we build a church or set apart a place of worship we do something which reaches far beyond the obvious significance of the fact. The whole world which God created has become a place where men have sinned; the devil has been at work, a fight is going on constantly; there is no place on this earth which has not been soiled by blood, suffering or sin.

When we choose a minute part of it, calling upon the power of God himself, in rites which convey his grace, to bless it, when we cleanse it from the presence of the evil spirit and set it apart to be God's foothold on earth, we reconquer for God a small part of this desecrated world.

We may say that this is a place where the Kingdom of God reveals itself and manifests itself with power. When we come to church we should be aware that we are entering upon sacred ground, a place which belongs to God, and we should behave accordingly.

Body and soul

The body has been prepared for the burial; the body is not a piece of outworn clothing, as some seemingly devout people like to say, which has been cast off for the soul to be free. A body is much more than this for a Christian; there is nothing that befalls the soul in which the body does not take part. We receive impressions of this world, but also of the divine world partly through the body.

Every sacrament is a gift of God, conferred on the soul by means of physical actions; the waters of baptism, the oil of chrism, the bread and wine of communion are all taken from the material world. We can never do either good or evil otherwise than in conjunction with our body.

The body is not there only, as it were, for the soul to be born, mature and then to go, abandoning it; the body, from the very first day to the last, has been the co-worker of the soul in all things and is, together with the soul, the total man. It remains marked for ever, as it were, by the imprint of the soul and the common life they had together. Linked with the soul, the body is also linked through the sacraments to Jesus Christ himself. We commune to his Blood and Body, and the body is thus united in its own right with the divine world with which it comes into contact.

Forgiveness

Judgement would hold nothing but terror for us if we had no sure hope of forgiveness. And the gift of forgiveness itself is implicit in God's and people's love. Yet it is not enough to be granted forgiveness, we must be prepared to receive it, to accept it.

We must consent to be forgiven by an act of daring faith and generous hope, welcome the gift humbly, as a miracle which love alone, love human and divine, can work, and forever be grateful for its gratuity, its restoring, healing, reintegrating power.

We must never confuse forgiving with forgetting, or imagine that these two things go together. Not only do they not belong together, but they are mutually exclusive. To wipe out the past has little to do with constructive, imaginative, fruitful forgiveness; the only thing that must go, be erased from the past, is its venom; the bitterness, the resentment, the estrangement; but not the memory.

Cross and incarnation

To understand the meaning of the saving death of Christ, we must understand the meaning of the incarnation. Each of us is born into time out of non-being. We enter a fleeting, precarious life in order to grow into the stability of Eternal Life. Called out of naught by the word of God, we enter into time but within time we can find eternity, because eternity is not a never-ending stream of time. Eternity is not something – it is Someone. Eternity is God himself, whom we can meet in the ephemeral flow of time and through this meeting, through the communion which God offers us by grace and love in mutual freedom, we can also enter into eternity to share God's own life, become in the daring words of St Peter, 'partakers of the divine nature'.

The birth of the Son of God is unlike ours. He does not enter time out of naught. His birth is not the beginning of life, of an evergrowing life; it is a limitation of the fullness that was his before the world began. He who possessed eternal glory with the Father, before all ages, enters into our world, into the created world, wherein man has brought sin, suffering, death. Christ's birth is for him not the beginning of life, it is the beginning of death. He accepts all that is inherent in our condition and the first day of his life on earth is the first day of his ascent to the cross.

Death and resurrection

The joy of the resurrection is something which we, too, must learn to experience, but we can experience it only if we first learn the tragedy of the cross. To rise again, we must die. Die to our hampering selfishness, die to our fears, die to everything which makes the world so narrow, so cold, so poor, so cruel. Die so that our souls may live, may rejoice, may discover the spring of life. If we do this then the resurrection of Christ will have come down to us also.

But without the death on the cross there is no resurrection, the resurrection which is joy, the joy of life recovered, the joy of the life that no one can take away from us any more! The joy of a life which is superabundant, which like a stream runs down the hills, carrying with it heaven itself reflected in its sparkling waters.

The resurrection of Christ is reality in history as his death on the cross was real, and it is because it belongs to history that we believe in it. It is not only with our hearts but with the totality of our experience that we know the risen Christ. We can know him day after day as the Apostles knew him. Not the Christ of the flesh, but the ever-living Christ. The Christ of the spirit of whom St Paul speaks, the risen Christ who belongs to time and eternity because he died once upon the cross but lives for ever.

Adoring the mystery

We must be prepared to find that the last step of our relationship with God is an act of pure adoration, face to face with a mystery into which we cannot enter.

We grow into the knowledge of God gradually from year to year until the end of our life and we will continue to do so through all eternity, without coming to a point when we shall be able to say that now we know all that is knowable of God. This process of the gradual discovery of God leads us at every moment to stand with our past experience behind us and the mystery of God knowable and still unknown before us.

The little we know of God makes it difficult for us to learn more, because the more cannot simply be added to the little, since every meeting brings such a change of perspective that what was known before becomes almost untrue in the light of what is known later.

Sources and Index

In the index below, the figures in bold type refer to pages of the present book. For the references to published works from which the readings are taken, abbreviations are used as follows:

CP: Courage to Pray and *GM: God and Man* (SVS Press); *LP: Living Prayer* (Templegate Publishers); *MT: Meditations on a Theme* (Dimension Books); *BP: Beginning to Pray* (Paulist Press).

SVS Press, 575 Scarsdale Rd.,
Crestwood NY 10707
Paulist Press, 997 Macarthur Blvd.,
Mahwah NJ 07430
Templegate Publishers, P.O. Box 5152,
Springfield, IL 62705
Dimension Books, P.O. Box 811,
Denville NJ 07834

*adapted

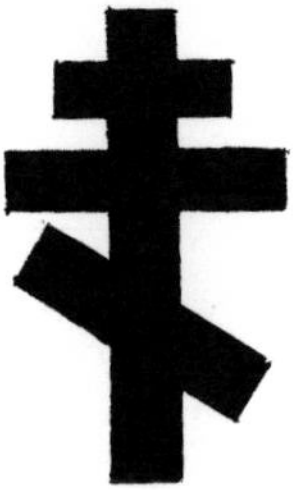

DATE DUE

JAN 19 '97			
MAR 3 0 1999			